ROMANIA!
Fantasy for Flute and Piano

DANIEL PAGET

Edited by Carol Wincenc

KEISER

Program Note

When my dear friend, the fabulous flutist Carol Wincenc, traveled to Romania in the early 1970s, she found an irresistible world of traditional music that included an enchanting repertoire for the *nai*, or panpipes. With roots extending back thousands of years, the nai consists of a graduated series of attached reed or bamboo pipes that are blown across their tops. Music for the instrument derives from peasant songs and dances (some of which have the characteristic limping rhythms that arise from the steady alternation of two pulses, one slightly longer than the other), and ranges from the hauntingly melancholic to the brilliantly virtuosic.

In 1979, in preparation for her Naumburg Award Recital at New York's Lincoln Center, Carol asked me to create a work for her drawn from this wonderful folk music. The result was ***Romania! Fantasy for Flute and Piano***, a duet suggestive of both the nai and the *cimbalom* (a kind of hammered dulcimer popular in Eastern European folk and other music). *The New York Times* noted that the premiere, at which Carol was joined by harpsichordist Kenneth Cooper, "raised the audience to heaven," a response which has been replicated many times at her subsequent performances of the work.

Daniel Paget,
Composer

Of all the musical gifts I could receive, nothing is as special as an original work written expressly for me! Maestro Paget's ***Romania!***, a brilliant "tip-of-the-hat" to my Austro-Hungarian heritage, showcases my deepest inner tzigane-style temperament. I have taken great care to select dynamics and articulations that allow the phrases to make the best use of the flute's capabilities, given the rich harmonic language typical of this part of the world. Filled with meltingly beautiful lyricism and dazzling technical gestures, this work has brought me years of enjoyment, as it will surely do now for all who have this beautiful new edition.

Carol Wincenc,
Editor

Commissioned by Carol Wincenc

Romania!

Fantasy for Flute and Piano

DANIEL PAGET

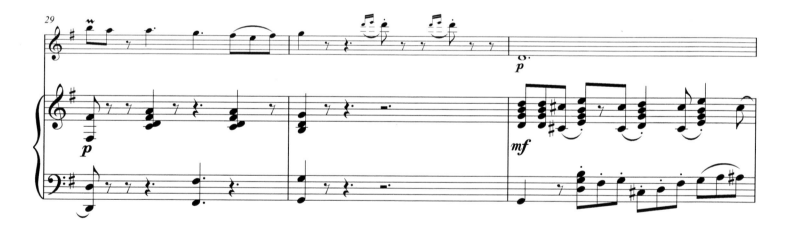

6

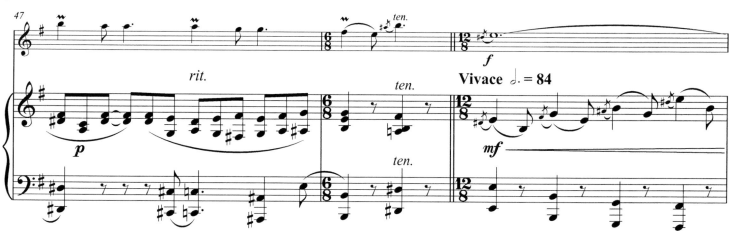

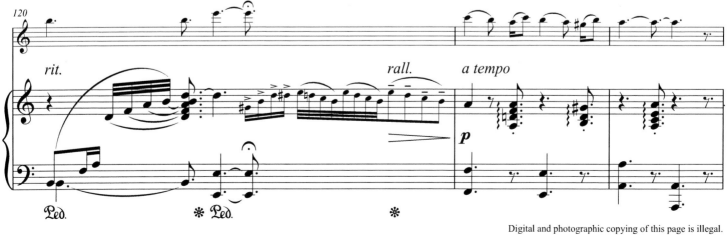

Flute

Commissioned by Carol Wincenc

Romania!

Fantasy for Flute and Piano

DANIEL PAGET

V.S.

Flute

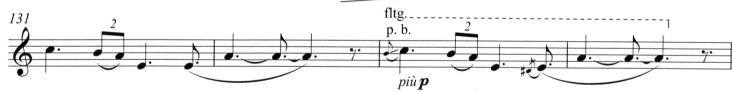

attacca

4

Flute

Flute

Flute

8

Flute

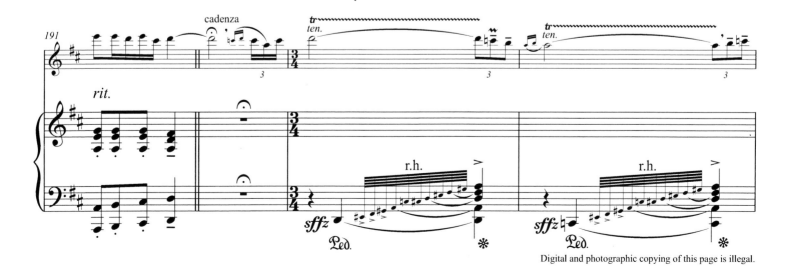

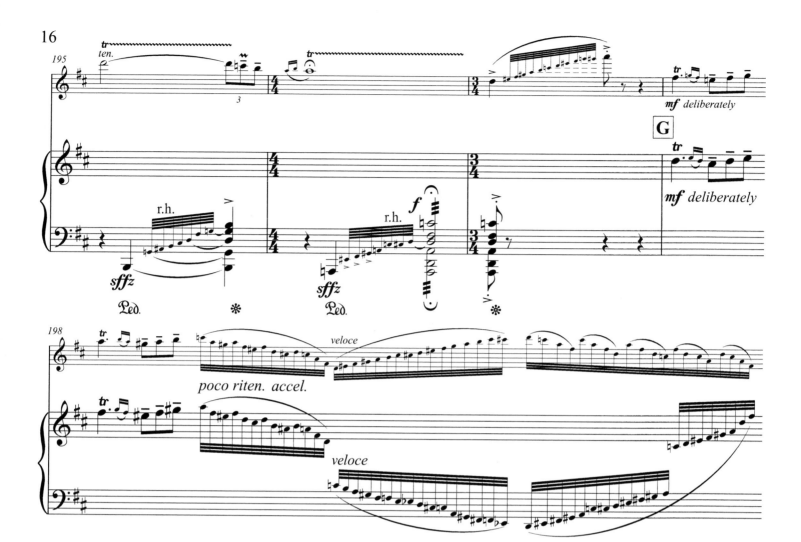

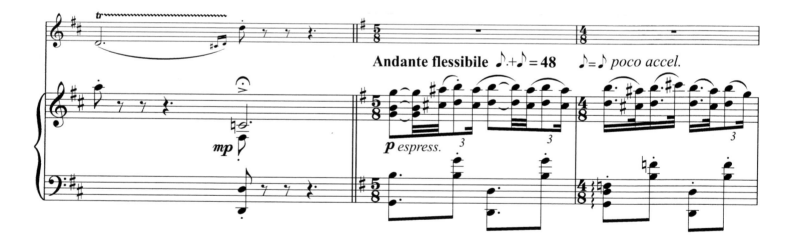

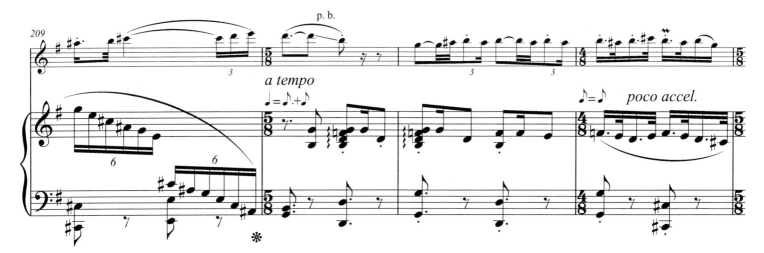

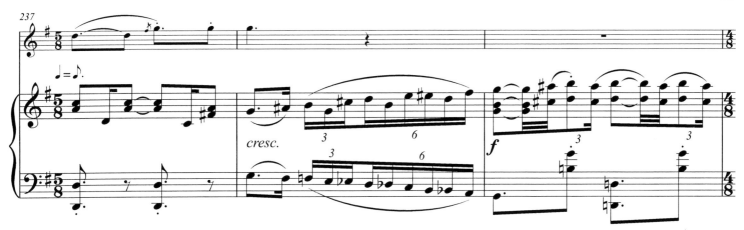

1. **Moderato** ♩ = 100 2. ♩ = 112

accel. sempre, poco

a poco

Allegro ♩ = 124

28